Kangaroo Paws

Kangaroo Paws

POEMS WRITTEN IN AUSTRALIA

David Ray

THOMAS JEFFERSON UNIVERSITY PRESS
Kirksville, Missouri
1994

Some of these poems were originally published in the following:
> Footwork: The Paterson Literary Review
> Fremantle Arts Review
> New York Quarterly
> Potpourri
> Southerly
> Sydney Morning Herald
> The Toronto Review
> The West Australian
> Westerly

The author is grateful to the University of Missouri-Kansas City, which authorized a leave allowing him to accept residencies at Australian universities, to which he is grateful for hospitality, particularly the University of Western Australia. He is also grateful for a Yaddo residency, during which some of these poems were revised.

Library of Congress Cataloging-in-Publication Data

Ray, David, 1932–
    Kangaroo paws : poems written in Australia / David Ray.
      p.   cm.
    Includes index.
    ISBN 0-943549-34-5 (paper)   0-943549-35-3 (case)
    I. Australia—Poetry.   I. Title.
PS3568.A9K36   1994
811'.54—dc20
                                  94-47568
                                      CIP

The paper in this publication meets or exceeds the minimum requirements of the American National Standard—Permanence of Paper for Printed Library Materials, ANSI Z39.48 (1984).

For Judy

Contents

"This is the flower which is so like Australia; none of your mountain daisy business about it, mind; no primrose or snowdrop racket; but a splendid, confident, audacious glory ... even the unpoetical Gropers claim the kangaroo paw as their national flower."
—Joseph Furphy, *Such Is Life*

"Such a vivid signal ...
a furred flower
green and scarlet."
—William Hart-Smith

An Outing in Sydney
At the Time of Gorbachev's Overthrow

Sunday we took the train, then bus
to get to Bondi; and to warm ourselves
for the beach we first stopped at a hole-
in-the-wall restaurant, had lentil soup

cooked and served by a fat Russian
woman who said, "They've tasted freedom
and will not let it go now." She stood
over us, watching us eat the soup

as if it were Freedom. She meant,
of course, grandmothers climbing up
on the tanks. She meant the three
young men crushed by the tanks,

young men now declared heroes forever.
(A statue of them might well replace
the tall bronze of Lenin, toppled.)
She meant the events last week

when words somehow got through
the thick skulls and helmets.
She sent us on our way
with an apple tart cut in half,

which we ate as we sat on a bench
above the sea, the curving Bondi bay
where surfers rode out to meet
each lashing wave, roll in the womb-

like swell. In a concrete pool
right below us, the Iceberg Swimmers
did laps in aquamarine. You got goose bumps
just watching. Then we walked

buskers—street
singers or
strolling
entertainers

the boardwalk, charging through the twang
of buskers and holiday makers.
Children charmed us as ever, and on
the far side of the beach two women

lay with their tops off as if to allow
the sun to make love to them. Perhaps
they were from the brothels, legal
in Sydney, and were advertisements

for themselves. Or perhaps they just
loved the sun. That's Freedom too,
we would say to those who object.
Everything was free that day

except for a few coins for this
and that. I have most of this on film,
by the way—the day we went to Bondi,
when People Power took a great many forms,

offered much to behold and try grasping
with mind—understanding and loving—
when People Power was palpable, rippling
through air, fired by sun and obvious everywhere.

BLUE MOUNTAINS

If you go out to Katoomba you can stay
at the Katoomba Hotel
or the Hydromajestic, or rough it
in the youth hostel or spread your swag

in the park. At midday you pay
to ride the gondola car
or head down in the tramway
crammed full of Japanese tourists.

Bright green parrots gyre round
your cage and their cameras. By the way,
we don't say Jap any more
despite what they did in Burma—

three hundred and six Aussies dead
every mile of their slave labor railroad.
Forget about that and every past evil
committed by anyone! Crane your neck

and gawk up where the gondola rocks
in the wind. They're all leaning
on glass, waving back. Point up
your lens, make a wish: that their cable

will break, fall, provide you a scoop,
infuse a thrill into this calm.
A lost rope from the old mine dangles—
slave labor there too, mostly coolies.

swag—bundle
of belongings
carried by a
swagman, i.e.
tramp or
hobo.

A Stroll in Sydney, After Reading Schweitzer

If Albert Schweitzer could take a stroll
with us and see the woman whose one mission
in life, it seems, is kindness to dirty pigeons,

he might well sigh and say, "We must leave
the incomprehensible uncomprehended."
He would know as well as you and I

that she dispenses her bountiful love
to the unworthy, that not even the clean
breeze off the sea can blow black soot

off these birds of the gutter, birds
that flock around the pensioner's cottage.
And if he should sit with us in the tea shop

owned by the friendly Greek, Albert too
would chat with another such human pigeon
and for the same reason I do, to comfort her—

for she sits in the corner weeping
and talking to herself, knocking atumble
again and again her stack of plastic bowls—

the rice pudding she'll take home—each
a full meal for her later—or so I suspect.
In the day's news and gossip she inserts

herself. "I am so happy," she tells us,
"the hostages are being let go. You see,
I'm a hostage myself." She goes back

to weeping a bit, for herself and others
in chains, then she asks me, "What war
were you in?" (Every man is presumed

to have been in at least one.) Then she adds,
"I'm a war hero myself." She wipes snot
on the sleeve of her frayed Persian lamb.

"So long as such suffering exists,"
Schweitzer wrote, "the compassionate person
cannot be at ease." But all I can say

is, "I see you like rice pudding." "Yes,"
she replies, glad we have spoken. "He puts
lots of nutmeg on top." And the Greek too,

leaning over his counter, has a smile
just for us, the unlovable ones of the world.
I think of Schweitzer, how they laughed

at him for saving the palm trees. The fact is,
we don't know quite whom we should save—
pigeons or sharks or ourselves—we who ruined

the rain, who walk out in it now at our peril.
Or the children of Baghdad, whom we left
among ruins, after our "smart bombs." "Any day,"

says an impassioned conservationist,
"a woman will come forward willing to take
an endangered little beastie into her womb."

I know I would save these old ladies of Sydney,
who live on rice pudding and tinned catfood.
I would save palms in the midst of a jungle.

To a Child of Baghdad

Our bombs may blast you
to a better life. You and your vivid parrot
may even change places. We give you
a chance, at least, to better yourself.

Who knows, you may be born beneath
a lucky star next time, maybe live
in our land of milk and honey,
and do some bombing yourself.

They say you'll die this year,
that our bombs did it—the power outage,
polluted water, that sort of thing—
but they're stretching a point.

If you knew these bombs you would love them.
We draw faces on them. We keep them spit-
shined and give them pet names.
And they are smart—that's how they found you.

Anzac Day in the Antipodes

A perceptive people chooses its festivals, its heroes and its memories wisely.

    —W. F. Mandle, *Going It Alone*

I had seen many men die horribly, and had killed many myself, and lived in fear most of the time. And it is terrible to think that it was all for nothing.

    —A. B. Facey, *A Fortunate Life*

April twenty-fifth is the day of remembrance.
Cenotaphs dot the landscape, war memorials
"sacred and sad," and there's a contest

of cemeteries. Old men walk in parade,
filled with pride, filled with sorrow—
"a day of remembrance for those who died

to keep our land free." Yet, so far away
were those lands—Australia, New Zealand—
they might have been free anyway—

with those sixty thousand lost allowed to plow,
to father their children—and some might well
have been better poets than those I find

on the shelves, in one dusty town
after another—towns with Aboriginal names—
each with fireworks to mark the Queen's

birthday. At home we have the Fourth of July,
and we too keep adding new wars to our list.
Only a few Aussies openly weep.

Anzac Day— Anzac is the acronym of Australian and New Zealand Army Corps. Anzac Day is a public holiday in Australia and New Zealand commemorating the Anzac landing in Gallipoli on April 25, 1915.

THE KNOWLEDGE

In Sydney we lived for three weeks
next to the police morgue.

We'd never have known
had our host not informed us,

for that building
was as blank as they come—

concrete blocks, windowless,
the lighting muted, nothing

to catch attention—and yet
once I knew, I'd wake

to the click of the gate-latch,
watch the delivery

in the back door, the box trundled
out of the van. Very discreet

indeed. But then I began thinking—
how our own bodies lay

on the same level, perhaps parallel
to those others—the man robbed

in his cab, shot in the head,
burned to a crisp—the pilot gone down

in the bush, flown back to town—
the Strathfield killer and all

his victims. They wound up there,
next door to us, confessions

night after night that the city
is far from gentle, that again

and again darkness is chosen.
And only the sponge, dipped

in vinegar, is soft
as it was on Christ's face.

THE PEDESTRIAN SUBWAY

Buskers down under are commonplace.
Many belt it out even at breakfast
when maybe it's still dark back home—
many who have no talent at all, yet
are down on their luck, must perform.

tucker—food

Maybe they've not had any tucker.
They are strumming electric guitars
and giving us songs of cowboys, sheep
shearers, jackaroos. Their intent faces
are free entertainment though it's cruel
to glimpse those lost in glum meditation,
who merely hum loud. We float past them
and their upturned hats holding a few coins—
every one a decoy, bait that's caught nothing.

jackaroo—a
novice on a
sheep station
or ranch

We know just how we'd do it, and know well
we are just one up-turned hat away
from this status, and sleeping on grass.
This morning a cellist holds forth with Bach
propped on a stand in front of Aboriginal
murals on tile—lizards and crocs,
the thorny echidna. But I pay the musician
no heed, no more than if Muzak were piped in,
waves of it over commuters and shufflers.

echidna—an
Australian
spiny anteater

It must be a mile to that light in the distance.
But beyond the fading *partita* I break
into tears because a man with only a dime-store
kazoo such as I myself might be able to play
offers the lilting refrain of *Waltzing
Matilda* and it follows me down the tunnel—

all those thousands of miles catching up at once
as if the wild sea breaking broke that fragile reef, me.

LOST

On my last day in Sydney I grieved
my lost blue notebook everywhere,

made fruitless foolish queries
wherever we had been. I kept getting

floors of buildings mixed up
since they have a different system,

walk in on Two, call it Ground.
I've got to sit down and get

centered more, I told myself,
before a car clips me. They drive

on the left, and I step out too soon
after a glance to the left,

then looking right. My German friend
was killed that way in London.

Others put cigarettes
out on their arms; I just write

my thoughts in blue notebooks,
then make sure I lose them—

ineffable grief I have suffered
time and again, sharing all

I am, my most intimate thoughts—
seeking them down alleys, since cops

always say, "They throw away papers—
they don't want them, Mate!"

So some stranger winds up
with those fragments and shards

I need in order to glue myself
back together—just to be real

like some kid in a fable
who doesn't want to be lost,

afflicted, abandoned, tossed out
on junk-heaps, scattered in alleys

or made the butt of a joke.
"Hey, listen to this one!"

In one notebook I grieve another,
in one city remember a dark day in another.

THE WONDERS

Yesterday's paper published the list
of the world's seven wonders, brought up

to date—the Golden Gate bridge
which so many have leapt off;

the Taj Mahal, which so many
have trekked to, beheld by moonlight;

the great pyramids, of course.
And then, would you believe it—

the Sydney Opera House, giant
scalloped shells like ears listening,

absurdly tilted—
though maybe it's transfigured

if you've heard Don Giovanni sing there.
And one "wonder" is included

that's an insult to the world.
I mean the Concorde—supersonic plane

that flies every day
a few wealthy fools over an ocean

with wanton damage to ozone,
skin of the earth. That *wonder*'s

a threat to the earth, to all life.
And it's contempt for mankind

to fly it day after day. I put
down the paper, leave off

adding up wonders. Let the rest
go. But I'll make my own list—

will top it with you, never fear.
Then green, green that's found everywhere.

FOR A GREETINGS CARD

It's the best year thus far—
so they would tell us.

In East Timor, when the bulldozers
head out of town, even the kids

know it's time for more mass
graves in the bush. Their playmates

disappeared, this year or last.
Chained to the wall for five years—

twenty-three hours and fifty minutes
each day—Waite is returned

with apologies. Even the rain,
dead for years, still kills,

drifting clouds laced with it.
In Sydney is calmly debated

the chance of Chernobyl
in suburbs, in sight of the sea.

Best year so far—not to be outdone
I fervently pray, by the new one—

closing in fast, gaining on all of us.

Waite—Terry Waite, the British hostage who was released after five years of captivity in Beirut.

LANDSCAPE AND SEASCAPE

All afternoon we debate the smoke,
at first a mere smudge on the horizon.
We thought it might have been clouds,
but then it grew less ambiguous,
caught light and glowed from within—
a thunderhead or mushroom cloud
like the bomb, enough sooty mass

to shadow the land behind us,
filter the sunlight. So we spoke
of nuclear winter—how little
it would take to leave man
in darkness. We were glad we sat
by the sea—a good place should flames
chase us. Yet we were troubled,

for we have long known there is no hiding,
long known there is no sanctuary.
Though this day's fire take its place
in the diary and is deemed routine
and benign, we will go on watching.
We are circled on all sides—as imperilled
as any tribe, nation, clan or race

we ever wiped out. Next time we are the ones
whose skins won't be left, and we know it.

A Sunday in the Dreamtime

"Teddy wants to go for a parachute fly,"
the small boy throws his koala around—
the third he's worn out, though Teddy's

renewed every Christmas. We are serving
our time on a barbecue ground, picnic site
over the river, the great cracked rocks

*Dreamtime—
the mythologi-
cal past of the
Aborigines.*

declared by Aborigines to be sacred—
a part of their dreamtime. We too
are in dreamtime, grilling our "bangers"

*bangers—
sausages.*

on the electric grill provided by Parks
and Wildlife—far more convenient
than fire made by rolling a stick in hands.

We look down upon purling waters, see
that the stones do indeed look like a snake—
also a tortoise, an octopus, even an elephant—

and the tree is elephant-hided. Sacred indeed
are these grounds intruded upon by the bitumen
car park—and us. No Aborigines prepare their grubs

*didgeridoo—a
musical instru-
ment
fashioned as a
long wooden
tube.*

wrapped in leaves in this smoke nor does the long
wooden tube of the didgeridoo offer its music,
our brains soon responding with alpha waves,

serenity—a sense that we're at peace
with this land, pleasantly lost in our dreamtime.
On a rock high over the swift waters

one of the boys about to fall in looks just
like my son. But there's no time for grief.
The Aborigines have one word for yesterday,

the same for tomorrow. We must live
in the present—one day or forty thousand
years as one, here with the tortoise

and snake, the crocodile I note just in time.
Yet a man can be caught with no teeth at all,
his own mind both gaping jaws and dreamy abyss.

Promises

It's the Australian plague locust
they warn of—a grasshopper
with red streaks on his legs

until he becomes a pure terror.
I think of the Mormons
in that old movie, beating them

with gunny sacks. "They'll come
in swarms, Mate, I assure you.
Don't open your mouth.

And don't show any green!
They'll go for anything green.
They'd eat up that sport coat in minutes.

The trick's to paint the highways green,
then when they zoom in, zap 'em
with spray!" And what else is offered?

Kangaroo paws blooming toward heaven.

The View from King's Park, Perth

"Have you seen the view
from King's Park at night?"
asked our host, giving us
a lift back to the flat.

We had not, so he drove
an avenue between trees named for men
fallen in the first world war—
still their most sacred.

Each of those thousands
of trees has a plaque
with the name of one fallen.
We stroll toward the obelisk

crowning the hill—white marble,
its base etched in black. We gaze
through iron bars, read the names,
so profuse they continue in shadow.

There are enough war dead
to fill up every space we devise.
And what else can one say
of such a place? Praise the view,

jewelled cars winding along
the Swan, the insolent skyscrapers
lit up. And behind us in shadows
the wise lovers, their infinite sighs.

Perched in Perth

As far as we could get, yet not far enough—
perched at edge of the ocean farthest
from our own. But cars swarm here too
and smog is being made as if

they have to ape and mimic what we have
at home—labyrinth of highways,
also madness of our guns. In Sydney
a man drank five cups of coffee,

brooding while his gymbag stayed harmless
at his feet, then he stooped down,
picked up his gun and sprayed the place,
killed eight or nine within a minute—

just like our crazies back at home.
It's Country Trains we want, to get
back where the trees breathe blue
and views include no sign of man at all.

Transperth

"We're in the densest center
of the least populated place on earth,"
my friend tells us. "We're surrounded
by desert and ocean. It thins out
right outside town."

So when I see a fellow human
get on a bus, I think: there's another one
making up that density—one of the tiny
pencil points comprising the bull's eye.

Perhaps I should tell them how special
they are. I can see they have not thought
that for a long time. They look downright
glum and humbled, these riders of buses,

despite the sailboats and windsurfers
out the window. A perfect and enviable
scene, many in the Third World would say.

Yet they always ask for a transfer
and when we take a look
in the Casino full of smoke and booze
and despair—much like Las Vegas and Reno—
a man tells me, "This is Perth's only playground."

THE MICROGARDENER

Almost as small as what's in a test tube
must be what this gardener peers down upon
this morning—one blade of thin grass growing,
or the turf's bald spot alone would please him.

Or one lone bloom! All day he sits transfixed
on his bucket, yellow as daffodils,
pulls weeds with slow but certain clutches—
very much like pulling one hair at a time.

He thins what's already damned slim pickings.
Clearly it's a labor of love—nothing
an observer would be moved to admire.
His yard is perhaps the least impressive

on our block, though by far the most tended.
But my standards may be too demanding.
I should applaud his half-handful of weeds
gathered by mid-morning, note that he's plucked

by mid-day a dozen mismatched pebbles
off his tiny rock garden, resettled
one spongy rock from an ancient seabed,
placed it just where it should go, at least

for today. Tomorrow it may be moved
back where it was—much like my last comma,
which I'm not sure that I need, though I may.
I admire his attention to detail,

though we'll neither one of us be asked much
about how we achieved effects desired—
and apparent to God at least if he
observes every beast at his labor. And me.

The Party

Oh perfect people, or almost!
We arrive quite late, no fault
of ours—and mostly to admire you.
We'd kill for such a home—

bull's eye window,
gleaming floors, verandahs
all around the front, a few fruit
trees and a thorny coral or two.

And breezy air blows through
from starry night.
It's a shame to shut it out
with stained-glass jarrah doors.

jarrah—an
Australian eu-
calypt with
reddish-
brown timber,
highly prized.

But we'd not let this mob
wander as they do here,
turn it into chaos.
Though half a world away,

this kitchen could well be
in the U.S.A.—our house
they herded into, smoked the air
like ham till it was thick

as smokeweed. Then too
it was jabber jabber jabber
from those who—believe it
or not—were paid for thoughts—

some days. They act
the passive fools here too,

thick as thieves. Just in time
I correct my navigation—

almost mistook her careerist
quiz for more than welcome
flirting. I'd love to see
her dance and wave thin veils.

A cigarette's tamped out
in the midst of French
bread buttered. Sliced meat
curls as it's smoked some more.

We leave before the picaninny dawn,
by which time kookaburras
have taken up the task, and also
magpies, those chattering thieves.

picaninny dawn—the approach of dawn, first light.

kookaburra—an Australian kingfisher with an abrupt, harsh cry suggestive of loud laughter.

GREENMOUNT

The happiest years of my life were spent in our home in Green-
mount in the West. My best literary work was done there. Our
joy brimmed over when our son was born. In those halcyon days
we could not have believed that for us the future had so much
misfortune.

—Katharine Susannah Prichard

We come to this cottage by chance, sit in the glow
of a pleasant fire, note the mantel lovingly carved
and the inlaid piano, cover over the keys. We ask

who once played it—the communist novelist, of course—
Katharine—for we are in the cottage she loved,
where she lived with her hero. Hugo had survived

the hell of Gallipoli, then Beersheba and Gaza—
his brother killed there. Hugo bore shrapnel for life.
He sorted out truth—how thousands of men had been
        betrayed

by the officer class, fools back far enough from the line
not to care much, and no good at all with their tactics.
But the light-horsemen had to charge the machine guns,

had to "get under" them. Hugo Throssell returned
with a Victoria Cross—one of the few accorded
Australia. Wherever he went he was hailed as a hero,

till his novelist communist wife talked him into
changing his speech–to an Anzac Day crowd waving flags.
He no longer believed in war, he announced,

and the crowd fell silent. He now had decided,
Hugo told them, the pacifists had been right all along.
The crowd booed him, and after that day one by one

snubbed him, crossed the street to avoid him.
Nothing he tried would work out, for the times
got worse and worse. He tried gold panning, real estate,

even a rodeo where his fame as a light-horseman
might lure them in. The crowd came but would not
buy so much as a cup of tea on the Sunday he opened

and the police arrived to say he could not charge admission
though he had mortgaged Greenmount for horses and
         saddles,
thrown himself into this effort. His communist wife

was in Russia, where they thought her novels terrific.
But Hugo stayed behind in this house, sent his son Ric
to live with an aunt. The bills kept rolling in

and the bankers refused his pleas, wished to foreclose.
Drought and Depression got worse—Hugo's, the world's.
The war had done something to his head, a throbbing

and nightsweats. Hardships were raging like war
but without the fanfare and fun. Topsoil blew into wind.
Again and again he toted the figures, sat up all night.

For the Victoria Cross a pawnbroker offered ten shillings.
The lights were cut off, and the phone would be next.
Kate's perfume on her letter just made him more heartsick.

The solution, when it came, was as clear
as those objectives faced in the war—waiting
till dawn for the charge. He still had his pistol,

had to wait for the light, get his will witnessed.
Otherwise, even this gesture would lead to defeat,
no solution at all. It took place on the verandah

over the slope where the kangaroo paw—unique
to Australia—trembles in breeze—a most marvelous
flower, illegal to pick. But the gardener gives us two.

Next morning I see how they glow, those paws
        clawing the sun.

ENVOI: TWO PAWS IN A VASE

for Hugo

Hugo's blood, and Katharine's
give these flowers their red—
paws of the kangaroo raised
in supplication.

His note read: "I feel
my old war head. It's going phut,
and that's no good
for anyone concerned."

Greenmount was saved,
where these stalwart stalks
were plucked from the slope.
On the verandah,

under the morning star,
warbling magpies were oblivious.
Hugo's blood dropped on the jarrah,
his service gun snagged on white lattice.

"The Union Jack on a bolshevik!"
someone objected at his funeral.
And Katharine came back from Russia,
to deal with all she had to,

raise their son Ric, endure torment.
This year the tenant at Greenmount
has named her babe Katharine.
The fount of life still flows sweet.

*Katharine Susan-
nah Prichard—
West Austra-
lian novelist,
born 1884,
married to
Hugo Thros-
sell. Their
home in
Greenmount is
now a writers'
center.*

43

FOR DENNIS

...words unspoken, ashes in a jar.

—Dennis Haskell

Amazing! —a man who grieved
for his father as I grieved
for a son.

He would gladly have leapt
into the grave, changed places.
And I, who always had

a hollow all through my chest
instead of a father,
stand amazed, impressed

as if at a grave's edge,
I who heard my father
like many another had died.

But only one son ever dies.
Immeasurable grief
swims the seas, all whales.

Never a minnow swims out
in that salt, where there's pain
beyond belief, and no relief.

44

ITEM IN THE LEDGER

In 1894, on June 26,
"removal of Mrs. Chalker's Brothel."

And no word at all
whether it was a good and well-run

brothel or not, and what the girls'
names were or whether they had boys too

or how long it served
before being removed. Nor do they say

who had complained, or why.
The script is elegant, though,

in black ink, slant calligraphic, glowing
as if with righteousness.

Moved down the street maybe?
No word of that, in the Ledger

of Fremantle. The rest of the page
is devoted to how many strokes

of the cat o' nine tails
in front of the jail—

mostly for drunken behavior—
some, I suspect, by those

who could not afford
a good night in Mrs. Chalker's Brothel.

God bless Mrs. Chalker,
who made it into the ledger,

into the history—propped open
in a glass case, to be honored

along with blue ribbons for all kinds
of things, and crosses earned at Gallipoli.

THE BICYCLE THIEF

A bicycle is a splendid thing.

—Ernest Hemingway

When something of yours is stolen
—your bike to be exact—
while you're lost in thought
in the library (you'd just be there
a minute—no need at all to lock
such a rusty old bike)—when something
of yours is stolen you stare
with amazement at the empty place
it should be. And is not! You confirm
by walking around the space,
and reconfirm, staring aghast.

Nor is there a sign
it ever existed—your bicycle—
though it could well be your woman,
your child, your home that has blown
clean away—it's Gone, Gone, Gone
with the wind. Or the bicycle thief.

In this case you can't believe it
because the old bike was rusty
and its fenders both rattled
and the seat had lost its spring
so that you felt every bump hard—
and the thief would already have
grease on his cuff, it's that kind
of bike. Nevertheless, you loved it
though you'd never have guessed
how much. And you try not to sob.
But you need to tell someone,

and try not to compound one wrong
with another—for on the way home
you see another bike left unlocked—
an offer to turn the day into profit,
not loss. But two wrongs don't
make a right, right? So you don't
ride off on that one, not quite so rusty.

But you've got to tell someone, quick.
And you do. But your wife's not mad
at the thief. Who left the lock off the bike?
And of course, you're mad at you too.
So that, Dear Reader, is why I'm turning
to you, and begging. Please, Dear Reader,
be gentle. You don't have to say much,
just listen. And I promise never again
to pass up a chance to lock up
whatever I can. I'm writing this confession,
in fact, in a lock-up dime-store diary
that's been blank since Christmas
two years ago and keeping the key
in a place I alone know, though I'll tell
you if we meet—unless you're the bicycle
thief—as I presume you'd confess to me.

Epilogue to the Theft

If you want to restore my faith
in human nature, I thought, walking my way home,
you can put the bike back. It was not quite
a prayer since a rusty old bike
is not worth a prayer—yet it was a strong thought
put out there, given to the mystical night air.

I'll gaze at that spot, I vowed,
whenever I pass. One never knows
when an attack of conscience might strike
a bicycle thief—perhaps in the night
when he'll sneak out to replace it in moonlight.

We grieve losses, yet rarely recover what's lost.
But the wish costs us nothing.
Think of Cinderella—or Dorothy and her yellow brick
road—and of all those whose brains are nothing
but song lyrics, circular tapes in their heads,
a kind of karma that permits nothing but best luck—
no purple rain, no loss in the night. When the boy
loses girl, he always recovers her,
                            at least in such lyrics.

And even the teddy bear and the tin man,
the witch and the scarecrow and that beautiful clown
Lucy and her drunk Desi live miserably ever after
on royalties and watch reruns far past midnight,
then sleep while there's nothing but snow
on that grey window into what once was the world.

The Goddess Lit Up

We zoom past a lit-up white building
of the Federation style, two-storied
with wrought-iron verandahs—an elegant
building with a sign in front—one word—
Aphrodite. "I went in there once
by mistake," my friend the driver tells us,
"I thought it was a Greek restaurant."

"Was it a Greek restaurant, Dad?" his son
calls out from the back seat.
"Yes, it was Greek," my friend calls back,
"but it wasn't a restaurant. Daddy
will tell you all about it some time."

But the boys begin jumping up and down.
"Tell us now, Daddy. Tell us now, Daddy!"

Once the goddess of love
is out of the bag
she insists at least
on being discussed with the boys.

EVIL ANGELS

Sometimes we don't know whether
we're going from good to better

or from bad to worse.
"The touch of the good angel,"

Ignatius tells us,
"is soft, light, and gentle

like a drop of water
making its way into a sponge.

The touch of the evil angel
is rough...like a drop

of water falling on stone."
My head is that stone

battered, disturbed
by more than one evil angel.

All night the rain
has been rough, battering,

thick as the darkness, fearful,
and my soul closed round.

It was indeed four o'clock
in the morning

and indeed it was night,
and my soul was in darkness.

Yet I would be that sponge
filling, always filling

with light, with such aery fluff
as angels bear with good will—

their burden—since they too
are battered through the night

when the night is as this one—
very bad, with battering rain.

A Glimpse of the Bride

The only gold you'll find this year
is a beer can bobbing close to shore.

Farther out, the beflagged yacht
of the honeymooners bobs, just a bit

more than the others. A pelican
swoops past their window. On these waters

Christ might well choose to stroll,
yet the only gold I pick up

is tossed-away baubles of litter—
gleaming foil and plastic to last

a thousand years. But thoughts
of consummation were, it seems,

premature. The bride's still on
the Yacht Club porch, also flagged

with pennants. She shoves her veil
aside and the best man lights

her cigarette. For one moment
in this gathering twilight

her face is aflame, glowing
with passionate intensity, throbbing

on the elegant verandah
of the Federation style porch.

I'm home by dark and leave the Swan
to gulls and rocking yachts,

to beds reserved and anchored.
And yet I bless each *liebeskind*

spawned on the football turf
and foreshore, where bodies twist

and turn, drowned or down for love.

DAWN

I hear the chorus. . .it is grand-opera. . .this indeed is music!
—Walt Whitman

One beat a day—

Sun strikes Ayer's Rock,
a red heart pulses once more.

A fool sees only stone
and not the throb eternal,

the Laws well in place,
the Wonder pounding again,

heart to heart, tireless
as waves striking shore.

Man strides his planet alone
only if he insists,

stands awaiting a word
spoken in tone and timbre as dull

as his own voice
might say it—hears neither silence

nor what's sung out in fire
or sea's *basso profundo*, other tongues.

Or this scene's red scream.

A QUIET DAY IN THE BUSH

In Western Australia everlastings
don't last very long.

Wasps hump orchids,
which smell wholly

female. Sundew
eats all manner of insects

and the honey possum's long tongue
performs cunnilingus

on more than one species—
very cunning indeed. The stinking

hakea—a shrub with gaudy flowers and woody fruit.

hakea is center for fat frogs
that grab flies attracted.

It's a charnel house in the desert—
no desert at all—and the jewel

beetle, aptly named since he glows
like a brooch, works his choice

of flowers, then fucks a yellow
reflector on a Toyota. All is quiet

today in the bush unless you get close,
hear the buzzing—or is it Mozart,

Brahms, maybe Vivaldi?—
with a live show, and us the voyeurs.

EARLY

There's a moment when the sun's diffused light
has talcummed the valleys, and the weeping willows
hang low but do not weep, and the dangers
so manifest and lurking in darkness are harmless
as sheets thrown over a chair in a boy's room,
no longer the feared ghosts of midnight. They are all
silvered over and silent. And I drink such a time,
such a landscape, I am so thirsty for it,
the harmlessness of that moment, those spider webs
on the box elder bushes glistening with dew.

THE ARRIVAL ON WESTERN SHORES, 1830

Stirling—Captain (later Sir) James Stirling arrived in Western Australia in 1827 to choose a town site, initiating British colonization of the Swan River estuarial area.

Hooked by Stirling's posters
scattered around London and Liverpool,
they arrived after long months at sea,
had rounded the Cape of Good Hope,
spent weeks on the Indian Ocean.

On arrival, got credit for sterling—
150 acres for each pound of it—
and could keep the money as well.
Too much land to dispose of!
Furniture too—so many acres
for a piano, a great deal for a plough!

After these immigrants trudged inland
abandoned pianos from England
littered the beach.

No schools for the kiddies
on coast or bushland—
much work for women,
plenty for men clearing bush.
Now that land's worth something,
no immigrants needed. But that year,
more went back than stayed on.

Today we stop by a green paddock
where spider orchids and spears
of blackboys sway in breeze.

blackboy—
Small grass tree with a thick dark trunk and a head of grass-like leaves.

The river we crossed
was a massacre site.
But survival's a wonderful fact—

58

on the grass three Aboriginal children
climb in and out of one another,
graceful and pliant as lianas or pythons—
three faces smirking up at us

as if they've become one great brown cabbage.
And there's music of grass trees.

We walk the suspension bridge, our lives
not at risk. But we wish for a moment

they were. We're stunned by absence,
this sunny scene emptied of far too many ghosts.

PARADISE AT DUSK

These families under the gum trees
are enjoying Eden, it seems,
and yet there was a Holocaust here—

and across that blue sea
the Timorese are shot down,
their bodies bulldozed into mass graves.

Like wallabies, like rabbits,
the Aborigines were hunted down,
captured for sport, lied to

when locked up. "This evening
we will have a big party,
a corroboree." But then their skulls

were sold to a London museum,
ten pounds apiece.
So who was most civilized?

Trust was betrayed, again and again.
I see their faces now, haunting the town—
a few standing for so many.

Their eyes bug out with old fear.
"A witness to violence is a victim
of violence." One massacre

quokka—a
small wallaby,
now rare, of
Western
Australia

lasts thousands of years.
And what are men who will pick
up a small creature—a quokka—

60

and use him for a football,
then throw him into a fire—
and laugh? They are heirs

of men who did that to men.
The wee beasties still cry out
in the night. Paradise

still burns crimson,
then the dark falls like a lid.
Darwin's grasp did not reach so far.

A Moment in the Bush

I.

While I'm still about
nobody touches that tree,
said the Aborigine,

pointing out the coolibah
casting its shade
on red ground. This is where

I was born—not long ago—
about fifty years. Nobody
gonna touch it. It was more

bushy when I was born—
my sole birthright, y'know.
And it's older than me.

II.

Another thing about my tree, Mate.
It's the one that they sing about.
This is the tree, Mate.

It's a she tree, Mate,
and she'll see me out yet.
They can bury me here

in sight of this tree.
It's a bit hard, digging
where she's got roots.

But as long as we're still
in her shade, the general area,
that's good enough, away

from them poisons. They use 'em
and they get washed down
to where the people are drinking.

It's my tree, Mate, and I don't want
her to drink none of that poison.
Her and me both, we don't want none

of that poison. I got to take care
of her, and she took care of me.
Like I say, I got born there in her shade.

A Chat Regarding the Next Water Hole for Miners

True knowledge only comes of death by torture in the country of the mind.

—Patrick White

White man speaks with forked tongue
they used to say, a fast
and flickering tongue.

Consider this conversation
between men of the mining company
and the Aborigines to whom—

due to a fluke in the law—
they must explain their intentions,
roll out their blueprints—

though with more than one gesture
and spoofing tone they imply
the plans are not all that important.

All we want to do, one says,
is drill one little hole, one
or two should do it. An Aborigine

asks if they would have to disturb
much rock—for we are speaking
of his grandfather. Not at all,

usually they drill no more
than three or four holes, six
at the most. I think we'll drill six—

holds up his fingers—that should just
about do it. Again, the Aborigines
have a question or two

though they have not learned
to distrust, perhaps, quite enough.
Anew the question is posed,

how many holes you got to do
to our grandfather here. A dozen
should do it, the white man says

in an offhand sort of way,
scrolling up his blueprint, brushing
a fly. You'll hardly know we are here.

There's a handshake
and then an initialed agreement.
We'll put down twenty holes then,

just to be safe. Then the Aborigine
wants to know if his people too
can use the water, if the bore is successful.

We'll see about that, says the white man,
my men will get pretty thirsty—
it's hard work you know, very dry here.

Later the Aborigine elders
pay a visit up to the cave,
squat around the pool that's been

at the same level as long as they've known—
eternal waters to them. They look
at a hand that's been on the rock

thousands of years. They pick up
a few bones as if to listen to them—
that jaw of a grandfather shot

in the massacre. It seems they know
where the bodies are *not* buried,
though the white man thought his fires

had disposed of them. It's not
the water, one Aborigine says.
But how many cups will they drink?

And what other holes will they want?

BLUE EYES

for Jack Davis

> *[The portrait] is a remarkable likeness, although not quite cap-*
> *turing the sense of isolation and sadness that drifts in and out of*
> *his astonishingly green eyes.*
>
> —Alison Farmer, *The Weekend Australian*

> *"I have purposely left description of myself till last. If you can*
> *imagine a tall, big boned, tousle haired brown skinned boy with*
> *big hands, big feet and blue eyes you would have a fairly good de-*
> *scription of me as a boy."*
>
> —Jack Davis, *A Boy's Life*

Jack Davis has green eyes, just like jade
or so *The Weekend Australian* claims.
But when they looked right at you, you said,
they seemed to be blue. Do bright eyes fade—

blue to green—maybe with fame?
Perhaps they'll change, then, back to blue
if the crowds become too much for him.
As a child he ate wild possum and kangaroo.

When Jack was five he ran to his mother.
"The trees are talking," he told her,
"a big one and this other little one."
"Smaller, you mean," said his mother.

"Yes," he continued. "The little tree
said *Mummy* and the big one, *What*
do you waaant?" She patted Jack's knee.
"Trees always talk when the wind blows."

Jack Davis—
Noted West
Australian
writer of Ab-
original
descent who
has published
plays, poetry,
and autobio-
graphical
memoirs.

And sent him out to gather the eggs.
My mom would have set me straight fast
though she too kept Wonder alive,
by teaching fear of lightning and thunder.

Whom to believe, *The West Australian*
or maybe *The Age*? Jack's mother or mine?
In the great Depression, Jack with blue eyes
or green and I with grey watched the swagmen

roaming the lanes and tramping the roads—
he in Australia and I in the States.
We did not scoff as other boys did. We'd have gone
along if we could have. And we gave them bread.

The Unmentionable

The Baron was playing something hard and ugly...like five-finger exercises but with more notes, oh! lots of notes in it...
—Henry Handel Richardson, *The Fortunes of Richard Mahony*

The Fortunes of Richard Mahony—Set in the late nineteenth century, this trilogy by Henry Handel Richardson (pseudonym of Ethel H. Lindesay Richardson, 1870–1946) is a classic of Australian literature.

One thing they dared not speak about then—
one among many—though life in the bush
was not lacking in whatever theme you might,
a hundred years later, choose to discuss.

A *short, sturdy little man, bronzed brown
with the sun* comes to visit. He looks almost
transparent, with *kindly blue eyes.* The pink
little faces find him intriguing. In return

he beams upon them. After dinner he plays
the piano and little Cuffy finds his mouth
simply smiled by itself. Transfixed, the child
thinks of running away, and his heart

beats too fast, *as if he had run... But the piano
didn't care; it went on and on...a dreadful thing...
he felt all swollen...yes, he was going to burst...
And then the Baron played little notes like the wind*

and sang funny songs in his ever such a funny voice.
And then this stranger asks the child, not the mother,
if he would like to be played to some more.
The boy gulps and bolts from the room, hides in bush,

humbled, he knows not why—something in this man's
attention and the music that somehow plays upon him.
Sheepish and shamed, the boy submits to their talk
about him. He must play for the Baron, says his mother.

Damned if he will! *But Mamma threw him a look.*
He will play for the Baron, as she turns the pages.
Cuffy counts flies on the wall. But the Baron sees
through this, like a mind-reader, asks how many.

The boy blushes, confesses it's twelve blowflies,
seventeen little ones. There's more talk
of music, and the Baron takes Cuffy's face
in his hands, turns it up. The brown bearded face

above him is solemn as the Baron kisses the boy
on the forehead, blesses *God's most precious gift.*
Later he insists that they walk in the bush.
"*Nay, we leave the little sisters at home with Mamma,*

and make the promenade alone, just we both."
Into the bush they walk, farther than Cuffy's allowed.
They sit on a log and the Baron takes
the boy's hand, looks at it closely as if it was funny.

He keeps the hand a long time, holding it, *his other*
hand on the boy's shoulder. Cuffy kicks his heels
against the log. He does not like having his hand held
or the Baron asking him questions. The Baron talks on

about things the boy does not know, and finds dull,
like being in church. He struggles, politely,
to wriggle his hand free. The Baron talks on about music
and weeping and suffering and fears in the night

that devour a man's peace. He has thoughts he can't say
to a boy, to one so tender. "*I have sung you*
of the nightingale, and moonshine, and first love...
all of which the Youth is full." He mentions

Shooh man and *knowledge that will soon enough*
come of pain. The boy slides away, hears the Baron say
he must give up all else for music. But it's time
to go home, and the boy breaks free, runs ahead.

A few days later a letter proposes that Cuffy
be allowed to go with the Baron. He will defray
all expenses. The parents are flattered—
such a high opinion of our child's gift—

from a connoisseur in music. It's delightful
he took a liking to Cuffy, will give him
a home, a career all based on his *musical faculty. . .*
ear, instinct, inborn receptivity—but they argue.

For the mother has an instinct as well, and bristles,
she knows not quite why. "Thank God," she says,
"I've still got my children. . . . I've got them
and I mean to keep them!" On the verandah

the boy tells his sisters, "Shooh Man"
and they reply "Shooh woman." They are laughing.
But the story did not always come out that way,
with the mother protective and wise and firm

with her instinct triumphant, not beaten down.
A great many angels grew in the bush, plump
and cherubic, delectable. And many a hunter
with musical calls stalked them. And many a mother

shuddered with some fear unmentionable. The Baron
had to find his Ganymede boy farther out in the bush.

Between the Sea and the Forest

In the souvenir shop we're invited
to share the guilt, cart away
heartwood, a piece of the forest—
a clock face, perhaps, of polished-up
jarrah, smooth as a mirror.
That's a rare wood. Or maybe a salt
and pepper set, also of jarrah.
Bowls are carved out of it, smooth
to the touch. Letter-
holders, little boxes, honey dippers,
and so on, all manner of gimcrackery.
I catch my breath, feel oppressed
to think of the forest hacked down, the blue sea
raided for pure trumpery, a sea horse
and coral for one's mantel, a giant conch
that will never be lifted to blow
the walls down—it *was* the wall.
In the presence of guilt so massive
I am numbed but polite—
a bourgeois who made his peace
with the Nazis. I am God's angry man
silenced, and humbly take leave
after buying something relatively harmless.
In the Ozarks it was cedar carved
into little outhouses or heart-shaped boxes
with scorched lids naming one's true love,
with a smell inside sweet and alive
even unto the seventh generation.
Clear cut and burned black to the root
are the ex-jarrahwood forests
motored through, to get home.

GULLIVER'S TRAVELS

It was a terrible thing men had done to the great tree.... She
dreaded the vengeance of the trees.
—Katharine Susannah Prichard, *Working Bullocks*

Above Perth in King's Park
near the lit-up obelisk
with names of the war dead

a great karri log lies
on blocks, a tribute
to the logging industry

of Australia. The single log
is nearly three hundred feet
long and six feet thick

and it's a wonder how
it was hauled out
of its forest. By no

means the largest,
the bronze plaque assures.
"And what's it used for?"

I asked, this hardest
and best of all woods—
nearly extinct now.

"Toilet paper," answers
my guide. "Most of it
goes to Japan as chips.

For toilet paper."
Next day I grieve not
the war dead, flowers still

left for them—over three
score and ten years after
their war. But the logs

I mourn—the Gullivers
men climb and crawl upon
and haul out of the forest

that we and the Japanese
may wipe our asses smooth.

THE HUMMING

In a godless time, I've heard,
men still scan heaven for signs.
Without any faith at all

they query the gossipy bird—
seek meaning in squiggly lines
in the dust, a jagged scrawl

that must reveal something.
They stare at etchings in rock
and the striations in petals,

wonder why blossoms cling
to one wave. Out of a flock,
they'll notice, one settles

close by, as if for a chat.
But take no notice of that
unless you live in a flat

and terrible time. You alone
know if you need such wisdom
as what is heard in the hum

given off in the heat of a stone.

A NOTE ON EVIL

What's evil, we get round to asking.
Dostoyevsky: a game enjoyed
by the devil, that old exile
from shabby gentility—girls
of a village taunting the peasant
to lick an iced axe, slicing the tongue.
He loves their pure enjoyment,
enjoys it himself in his travels—
would love to see an iced axe
spinning in space, the giant mirror
Hitler so wanted to tilt
at the earth as a death ray gleaming.

Augustine could suffer self-reproach
for a lifetime, from stealing one pear.
Others stole beauteous breasts
or candlesticks. And rotted in one prison
or other, broke their heads on the rocks.

Australia was no Terra Nullus
as Captain Cook claimed—empty land
he could have for nothing. Big eyes
watched, and he saw them. No one
was there, claimed his whites,
yet brought gifts of poisoned flour
and in New Zealand the Maoris too
were given blankets covered with cholera.

brumbies—
wild horses,
especially
those de-
scended from
runaways.

Hunted down for sport, blacks were driven
into pens like wild brumbies today.
Babes were thrown into fire screaming.
The guest of empire would admire

an Aboriginal group—friendly souls
grinning—spot a choice head and say
"I'll have that chap's head before dark."

And he did. Bones were sold
to London museums, ten pounds per skeleton.
"Uncivilized," claimed the white man
who boiled bodies to bone. What he meant:
they did not bury their dead,
making his civilized task easy.

Even today the weekend drunk on Rottnest
throws a quokka on his campfire—
suffering creature the size of a football,
used also for that sport in drunkenness,
the ball squealing its cries, flailing
space, helpless paws clawing.
And evil was childhood, their not giving a damn
                 when we hurt so much in the night.

DESIRE

This evening I feel that I have dismissed all the reproachful
thoughts I harboured, and in consequence have made a long
poem. . .

—Po Chu-i

I fall in love too easily.

—popular lyric

Such emptiness, devoutly to be wished.
Achieved by the Chinese poet and by countless

others obscure forever. Their hard-won peace
they took with them, leaving a deep silence.

And I have none of it. Each was denied
what he most wanted, I'm sure. And even

she, the object of desire, hungered for what
she could not have. Why do our minds invent

perfection? Can I not at least imagine
the goddess with bad breath? Lust is mortar

of pain, the wall we build around ourselves.
And how indeed, in that prison, we cower

and shiver, comfortless. Brick after clay brick
we lay down, walling ourselves in. Yet did not

Beauty command us? Should we not worship her?
Oh, Beauty and the pain of not having you!

Beauty and the pain of not touching you!
Beauty and the pain of not falling to my knees,

kissing your thighs! Again and again I embark
from your shores, alone except for Po Chu-i and Buddha—

not much comfort at all—and no substitute
for your softness glimpsed and your eyes burning.

Go in peace. Give what you may where you may.
I deserve nothing. I kiss your hand across oceans.

LUNACY TRIBUNAL: THE POET FRANCIS WEBB PLEADS FOR HIS FREEDOM

...that other form of madness by which men, in an act of sovereign reason, confine their neighbors and communicate and recognize each other through the merciless language of non-madness.
—Michel Foucault

Francis Webb—
An Australian
poet (1925–
1973) who
spent his last
years in a
mental
hospital.

Bugger your thoughts of my oddness.
You've scanned every word of my letters,
pointed out madness—on all sides of us,
I agree, and hanging like dust in the air.

Madness indeed, it afflicts and affects me,
even as you—no more, though. I see
suspicion clouds judgement—not merely mine.
You too have known, surely, storms of harsh

judgement, how trees soon lash and cut
at the innocent's face even as lightning
impales him—I mean your wars, Man,
in blunt speaking. Just look at them,

begun with self-righteous scorn
such as you're predisposed to, urge
in my case. If you, grey grim men
and gaunt She-wolf, knew such a scorn

turned upon you, it would wither you
utterly. You would curl up and die writhing.
Leap more softly to judgement, I say.
If you won't let me go—like parents possessive—

ticket of leave—a
convict's
parole paper

deny me my ticket of leave—I'll enact
madness indeed. You see, Sydney awaits me,

with a thousand glints on the harbor.
Or the bush—peace to be found there

beneath blue haze, perfume of the gum trees.
I'll not cringe, gentlemen, nor offer fake gleam
of friendship. A 'case-sheet broad
as your head,' you intone, and my poems stuffed in—

merely more data, like lab work—good for nothing
in your world, seen as mere symptoms.
Self-murder hinted, you charge me,
yet it's you who would murder me, have done so

before, set my corpse jigging, limbs jerking.
Madness is made here, all impulse for good stilled.
Only that bird out the window seems alive here.
You hold me down. Damn you. I'll float out

the window, climb into clouds, bank like a plane.
Or angel. Loony, you say, who could not yourself
write one tinker's dam's worth of line nor suck
Mother Moon, know she could serve you as well.

She helps who bows down or gets on his knees,
offers his soul to be moved. Tides swell in men.
Faithless ships sink. With a man it's his head
that's a dark stone unless aery and lifted to heaven.

Discuss me, will you, even as I watch?
I'm appalled—nay, amused—by your rudeness.
In the interests of whom? —State you serve?
Stamp my plea DENIED to defeat me, play

your wizard role out? Sanity not proved,
you declare. But which of you has proved his?
You, Madame? In these walls such proof
is not likely, perhaps not even possible,

though I've slowed and measured my words,
fought back all metaphor. (You suspect brightness,
words not dulled and honed down. You stifle
all music.) Damn you, your flatness of language,

your barbs of cold reason, iced thorns.
Of course I'd return here if troubled, of that
I assure you. I'd return to get balanced,
brought back to my senses, calmed.

You'd have me not read, and that I've agreed to.
The Pope himself asks nothing less. Sneak reading
was never my forte. My problem's the writing—
glimpsing a poem, snagging it in mind's net

just as your electrodes caught me—in silver
wire, beauteous, fire leaping within—
though they provided no cure, you decide.
Where's your faith? I endured all you prescribed,

should deserve to go free. I writhed on your wires.
Messieurs, Madame of Wisdom, grant me leave!
I'll grin for you, but wish to go free, never again
be immured here—be pig, be rat to test wonders.

When straps are undone and graph's calmed,
please let me go. Oh Fathers of Freud,
though you worked no marvels on me. Time spent
in prayer between sessions of torture

did far more to heal, at least till you probed.
John Stuart Mill: Ask a man if he's happy,
and he will forthwith cease to be so.
Have you not read him? Not honored here!

Nullarbor, indeed—not one tree in this gulch,
not one bough's shade on this sand. O foolish wisdom,
deaf and blind, that sees no fire, hears no Requiem
intoned by winds loosed in the ruinous canyons.

Nullarbor—
The Nullarbor
Plain is a vast,
dry, treeless
plateau in the
Southwest of
Australia.

Worst dreams led to you, to this worst here and now,
to more years monastic. Yet rim of this world is fringed
as if with lace, and a passionate heart heaves.
In that roseate distance my lost land grieves her least exile.

The Hemlock Society

She helped herself along—
with a few pills tucked away
for such an occasion—

'a very brave woman,'
out of it now,
not wanting to become

'a mere vegetable,'
'a burden to others.'
What are the years

that they lead us only
to this, the hemlock?
And no one believes it

when you say
you are ready,
have no regrets.

They themselves plan
to hold on
more tenaciously—

even while wilting
to flummery,
even while adding

ten tons of stone
on the daughter,
ten on each son.

My dearest, make sure
our subscription's
paid up, and keep

the stash handy.

HOMESICK

I've got to get hold of *The New York Times*
or sit in McDonald's a while
or walk through Woolworth's—

Is it not a wonder they have such places
half a world away?—
or I must find a James M. Cain paperback

and again figure out
why the postman always rang twice,
recall John Garfield, Lana Turner

in an embrace so passionate
that I still hold my breath and fear
that her husband will walk in. Or hear

on the radio news
the report of yet another—this one
in Texas. A girl tells us

Bush—This
simple word
for the forest
or country
areas, often, in
Australia and
New Zealand,
seems to take
on metaphysi-
cal overtones.
It is the focus
of primal
fears and dark
energies, and
of immeasur-
able distances
and confu-
sions of
direction.

in her drawl heard round the world:
"He just opened fire at random
and shot and reloaded

for at least half an hour."
Texas was never safe,
but in Oz this sort of thing

is like importing sharks
or lugging in tigers
to live in the bush with the crocs.

Without Words

Words never do it.
The hand on the belly
does.

But Oh, the wait
until midnight—
dreadful.

Nothing but words
all day,
worse than crows,

raucous, never saying
what they were
meant to,

never touching
the belly,
making calm,

bringing a breath
to a new dawn,
and hope.

THE LEPER

Be silent. Sorrow is a leper.

—A. M. Klein

Forgive me if I breathe a word of this,
if I have said his name again
or strayed—despite my vows—
into that futile prayer... *If only...*
or *If I had it to do over again...* I do not,
and even in silence should not retrace
regret nor chant the long list subjunctive
or wake with a way this time to avoid
that death absurd and unpredestined,
life offered to Nada and thrown to Chaos,
what would have been, was, a gift we dare not
think on, who counsel our love to die and be still.
And thus on a day calmed *ad nauseam*
with green forests in place and blue mountains
not trembling, far over the islands and oceans,
forgive me at breakfast and absolve me at lunch
if I sob or speak out my grief so offensive
to all industry, to that silence bleached white as bone.

CLIMBING THE TREE

Timor mortis conturbat me.

Touring Australia, doing the tourist things—
a descent into the jeweled cave, all lit up
with giant tree-roots piercing the ceiling,
having augered deep. They cracked rock
and kept going. And the guide takes us deeper
as I think of the womb, how unpleasant it was,

how unhappy my mother was even then
and how we both were assaulted, struggled, fought
for life. Wet walls gleam and alabaster
glows here too, as of tombs. We emerge safe
in the light and I am greatly relieved,
still panting, gasping for air, terrified.

Later the same day we stop at the Gloucester tree,
a great karri named for the Duke because he once
paid a visit, though he did not climb it
as you do in the dusk—hand over hand far up
in a spiral, then waving from the tower aloft.
The tree is like the mast of a ship. You both sway.

The cave was enough adventure for me. I sit
on a bench with a wife who complains—her husband
should not be climbing the tree, not at his age.
"In the morning his legs will be mush," she says.
And I think what a good job Mother did, teaching me
fear of everything under the sun, all she too

was afraid of, ever the child. Everything under
and over us, everything known—and the unknown as well.
In dark or in light fear was given *carte blanche,*

always had its way with us. And we were afraid
of each other, it goes without saying. What a waste
it has been, a lifetime of fear. Would it help,

I wonder, if I returned, made myself climb
that Gloucester tree? Or is it too late to change—
there's another fear added. Trembling,
I greet you, grasp your wrist, feel a pulse
not even quickened. "It was fun," you say.
"You ought to try it." Yes, indeed. And bless

every spider I've killed and the darkness
I stayed awake to watch and waters and sky
that not once have betrayed us. Not yet.

SIGHTSEEING, THE SOUTHWEST

The survivor must endure the stigma of merely surviving.
—Terrence DesPres

We sat by the lighthouse and watched
the two seas mixing, waves crashing in
from the Indian Ocean, the Southern.

And joked that if we did ourselves in
one of us might go to this ocean,
the other to that. We decided not

to try it, not today. Instead we took
the cave tour. There too it would
have been simple, slipping away

from the crowd, into one of the dark
tunnels. There was barely enough air.
To emerge again into sunlight

was a rebirth, a joy for a moment.
We gasped, were stunned by the brightness;
then after lunch you insisted

on climbing the Gloucester tree, sixty-one
meters high and swaying. One slip and down
you'd have plunged to my feet. I sat on a bench

and trembled, knowing all too well how hard it is
to resist temptation. Though I have put down
that Woolf in me who howls to walk into the river,

put down that Plath in me who laughs
at the thought of my head in the oven—
my work heeded at last—it is still hard

to leave the scars where they are—
and pass up even the drink the Thomas
in me begs for daily, doubting the reasons

I give for this lusterless regimen
which keeps us bourgeois and alive
one day at a time. Now and then

the dark world glows as if it is worth,
after all, sticking around for—
though I still envy the dead we would die for.

THE OBSCENITY

You, you, you writer!

—Ernest Hemingway

In Australia, writers
are born to it—grit
and bush being their theme—
Lawson in a tent by a gold dig,
Prichard in a cyclone raging.

But it was Erskine Caldwell,
an American, who created old Ty Ty—
as obscene a man as ever was born.
Hole after hole Ty Ty dug
in his own yard, seeking gold

he was sure had to be there.
He made a fool of himself again
and again, undermined his own house
until it tilted into a crater.
His land was pocked with his failures.

His obsession was deadly,
worse than his lust for Darling Jill.
Sight of her made him want
to get down on his knees like a dog,
so he said in his obscene and toothless lust.

And again and again Ty Ty broke his promise
to God, having promised Him the gold found.
He kept moving *God's Little Acre*,
like a writer refusing to share
so much as one tenth of his royalties.

Henry Lawson—Australian author, 1867–1923, who wrote many stories and poems about life in the bush in the 1890s.

Even so, writers blight land
with their visions, leaving slag heaps,
craters, wastelands hollowed out.
Toxic wastes of their labors
fill chartless pools, rainbows

gleaming on scum of it. And writers
never leave off, no matter how much
damage they've done, how much gold
they've failed to find—for God
or themselves. Thus the birth of one

bull dust—fine,
powdery dust,
as from out-
back roads.

causes so much pain screamed to high heaven
that you can hear it for years in the winds
over goldfields and islands, deserts and seas,
and taste it in bull dust of tenements
                      long-since razed to oblivion.

INTERTEXTUALITY
for A. D. Hope

A.D. Hope—
Australian
poet, born in
1907.

Such a simple folk tune it was
that inspired Beethoven's *Kreutzer*
Sonata—three beats with no pause.
Tolstoy heard it after an oyster

dinner one evening and it seems
he had a physical reaction—
vivid as if in his wet dreams.
Waltzers sought crude satisfaction,

horizontal, down on the floor.
Ah, how sensuous, hypnotic.
In his head he envisaged a whore
who offered love metronomic.

But *post allegro, andante.*
If you tire of Tolstoy, try Dante.

FREMANTLE

We sip our cocktails out on the terrace
of the penthouse, let the sunset
take place over the sea—a good half
hour's show this evening, an expiring

glow you can almost hear. Down below's
the lee shore deemed most dangerous
to shipping. We see nothing now
but a few yachts coming in from their day

of sportsfishing—the sort of thing
that might have brought Hemingway here.
But if we'd been sitting right where we are
at certain other times we might have seen

the great ships go down one at a time—
those of pirates, those of pioneers,
those of tea clippers. We watch the smooth
waters now and see not a single mast,

not even one hand, going down.
I peer over the edge of this penthouse
just to make sure no whale's being dragged
through the hole in the rocks

toward the market for blubber and oil.
And all the fat singers have left not
one note trilling, out of leviathan lungs,
and their corsets of baleen are in the museum.

Sunday Morning in Oz

There is so much pain.

—Ford Madox Ford

Fremantle beach—stone roundhouse
of old sea-watch, mast strung taut
like a sky-harp for tourists
to pluck with their minds

above great cliff-face bored through
for whales to be dragged—
every one welcomed, dismembered
by the rusty flanging, hacking,

slicing machines found now in the museum.
An iron gate swings on the tunnel
as if it's a jail—of shadows—
from which emerge a red-headed group

seeking their father. "Have you seen
an old drunk sleeping it off?"
She notes in my hand a can of Jim Beam
and Coke. "Just picked it up,"

I defend my poor image, though for sure
there but for the grace of God go I—
many a midnight's haven sought
against driftwood, salt logs sodden.

Flotsam of a man, yet they are seeking
him, old barnacled whale beached.
This loving harridan with hair hennaed
desires him, and would hug him to bosom.

These kids with fiery red curls would leap
up to him. One child has her own babe
held in arm and he too seeks his captain.
All this crew have his blue ocean eyes.

Could I be the loved father sought, just
this once? Or join them—I, Telemachus—
to seek him! An old man sits in shade
of cliff-face, reading the news.

But he's not the right man. These young
crying out for father bear that glum
mask my own son wore, who licked foam
off my beer. Now another calls out:

"He's been here, Mom, this sandal's
size nine." The boy holds up a blue thong.
Murdered by cannibals! I look up and see
only that cross strung taut against sky,

on mast of no boat, sailing nowhere fast.
Full weight of the dark sea rolls our way.

The Fortunes of Richard Mahony

So what's he doing now, Mahony
who took his wife and children
on the Grand Tour again—this time
to do it right? Presumably he's not

as foolish as I was—therefore
will not make *those* mistakes. And yet,
it seems, he left his money in the hands
of someone who absconds. In Venice

he gets a cable, RETURN IMMEDIATELY.
MOST URGENT. So he dashes off, boards
the first mailboat, will have no peace.
His fortunes are lost, kissed good-bye—

down the bottomless drain of perfidy.
His accountant is off for a new life
in America. "I guess it happened often—
that sort of thing. In *Terra Nulla*

you'd better watch out who you trust."
Indeed, I think, turning to face
the squalid papers of a misspent life—
one that makes Mahony's sad course

look like one unbroken upward ascent
of triumph—such a career as Professor Olson
drew with squeaky chalk on the blackboard
where brash light fell upon us as if blocked

Terra Nulla—
An uninhab-
ited land; a
legalism used
by Captain
Cook and
early settlers to
justify land
grabbing.

by prison bars, not the mullioned windows
of the Ivy League or Chicago. Far far West
of Melbourne I mourn the fortunes
of Richard Mahony, and more than one of my own.

D. H. Lawrence at Thurroul

with apologies to Joseph Davis

It is well-established
that when D. H. Lawrence
and Frieda took the ferry
to Manly, then the tram

to Marrabeen, to inspect
vacant houses, no third party
rode along with them, also
that their search was quite

unsuccessful. It can indeed
be proved that they rode
back half a dozen stops
to Collaroy and had tea

with a man named Scott
and that Scott's bungalow
was called Hinemoa,
overlooking the beach.

It can safely be assumed
that the great novelist
and Frieda looked out
upon the sea as they sipped

their tea, served either
with scones or with biscuits.
The tea was undoubtedly
Chinese jasmine, confirmed

by checking the bills
of lading at Sydney
for the weeks prior
to their visit. No record

exists of whether host Scott
offered dinner but a man
of his standing would not
have refused so distinguished

a pair his warm invitation.
We know for a fact, though,
that after the Lawrences
found their rental cottage

in Thurroul the novelist
had his red beard trimmed
by a barber—George Laughlin,
who recalled Lawrence

as "a morose-looking fellow."
Laughlin's shop was levelled
in 1985 to make room
for Housing Commission units.

Leaving the barbershop
smelling of the bay rum
Laughlin was known to have used,
Lawrence would have noted,

directly opposite, an octagonal
building which served for decades
as a waiting room for steam trains.
At "Wyework" he worked through

the winter, taking advantage
of off-season rates. When he
and Frieda took their walks
on the beach we know they walked

South rather than North.
They saw the bi-wing sightseeing
plane skimming the sea, for mention
of the aircraft is made in a letter

expressing a good deal
of bitterness that they could not
afford the three shillings fare
for a ride—a great loss

in that we would then have
his description of the town
and bush beyond from the air
as well as, one suspects, mention

of those sights familiar
to the townspeople but left out
by Lawrence—the strangely neglected
rail yards, the locomotive

depot, the brickworks and quarry.
We know too that Frieda was happy
at Thurroul, expressing her pleasure
that farmers gave her three pounds

of butter for every two paid for,
three pints of milk rather
than two. She thought it amusing,
however, that the locals

used suitcases as shopping bags
and that peddlers came to her door
with cabbages and rabbits in theirs—
opened up on the verandah

which had not yet been enclosed.
There is still work, however,
for scholarship—the mystery, e.g.,
of Lawrence's hat—lost

to a high wind. He nearly
got drowned—or so he believed—
wading in after it. The hat
has not yet been recovered.

And there's the question too
of whether, when Lawrence mused
over the town, what he saw
through distant open doors glowing

were electric lights or candles,
since both were quite common.
"The township looked its queerest
as dusk fell," he wrote,

which would lead us to conclude
that he was confused on the subject.
With more certainty we can date—
sometime between June 21st

and July 9th, most likely the Fourth—
the great man's trip back to Sydney
where—we can be sure—he paid a visit
to the Zoo, for there he saw

the kangaroo that inspired both
a scene from and the title
of his novel in which we find long
descriptions of birds and jellyfish

because he could not afford
a guidebook containing their names.
The year after David Herbert
and Frieda Lawrence lived at Thurroul

the town's first cinema theatre,
the Arcadia, was built across the street
from the Church of England. Had they stayed on
they'd have seen some interesting films.

THE DEADHOUSE

deadhouse—
Room at-
tached to a
hotel in which
the drunks
could sleep it
off (from *dead-
house* morgue)"
G. A. Wilkes,
*A Dictionary of
Australian
Colloquialisms*

These are not the children of Brazil
roaming the plaza, picked off one
at a time by death squads

but the children of Australia
sold a few stubbies, wine coolers,
pinch bottles, not to forget cigarettes

cradled in arm to the darkness
broken by bonfire, creak of timbers
torn loose from the old house. They die

for a certainty, they die for an industry,
they die because nobody cares and they prove
it again and again with each crash or fall

on the tracks or the slow rot of liver.
They prove it with vomit, with head in bucket
or toilet. They prove it by waking

with strangers. They prove it by death
of each brain cell—a galaxy gone
over a weekend. They prove it by flipping

through magazines, by glancing at signs
under spotlights and on walls of the stadium.
They prove it by the glib, easy tolerance

everywhere, by the genial face behind
the raised glass, and they prove it by cash
and keys handed across without question.

Not once in their lives has anyone cared
enough to say No. Somewhere in darkness
a father crawls through glass on his knees

to save one child from the death squads.
Too easy, we say, in our more civilized lands.
We will claw them back from the sky, pray

them back. The Aztec sun god drank blood
as if it were beer. Aussies give him six
thousand a year, think nothing of it,

onyx knife plunged deep again and again.

FREO

With hangover hurting he will wake miles from Freo
thinking how cold that wind from the sea felt, although
it was gentle, that sea breeze. And all in his mind,

the rest of it—the convicts transported for life.
They still rattled their chains and the ghosts of whales
were weeping. And yet, he was only walking
in moonlight down the street, in old Freo.

A Moment Shared in Australia

An Aussie remembers his stay in the States.
Two decades ago, almost, coming across
De Snodgrass weeping as he leaned

against a wall. "Why do we do it?"
he blurted out through his sobs.
"Do what?" said the Aussie.

"Berryman," Snodgrass explained,
"what he did in Minneapolis,
off the bridge," and held out

the paper, January 7, 1972—
at least that's the date recalled
at this distance. And I too

was stunned by that ice, river,
bridge, John Berryman falling
as if he'd driven the scene

into our skulls, though my morning
news was in Spanish that year—
for we had fled into Mexico—

seeking, hurting, just
as we do now in Australia,
where the bloody history

of American poetry is recalled
in fragments, one sharp piece
here, another there. Now and then

we are turned to as survivors,
asked for an eye witness account
of some of it—bloody history

indeed—poet uncles with pistols,
poet aunties in straitjackets,
others in nightgowns babbling,

nursing their wine, while over
their heads scream the jets
writing their version, too, for the muse.

JACK

In Australia a scholar tells me,
"We're undergoing a Renaissance
of Kerouac"—it seems they love
the guy—
                    and I think of Jack
slumped in his worn-out chair
down in Florida drinking
and smoking himself to death,

with sullen eyes watching
his mother move around the room,
yelling "Stella" at her,
like Marlon Brando in *Streetcar*.

Stella would bring him
his drink and his smokes.

And now and then
in the rocking Florida twilight
Jack would lean forward and hug her
around the hips, pressing his face
against her fallen womb.

"Go won, Jack," she would say,
her hand on his hair,
"Let it all out," and Jack
would weep enough for both of them.

Then Stella would push him away
and make her rounds of the room,
tipping out ashes, picking up bottles.

LUNCH WITH AN AUSSIE WRITER

Literary is like no other gossip.
It thrives in every climate

—like kudzu, like spinifex,
like the smelly hakea or mangrove,

like sand burrs with lots of fleas clinging.
He tells me about the poet who got drunk

and beat up the reviewer. I love it!
So I tell him about my old buddy Nels,

who wrote *The Man with the Golden Arm.*
He got a bad review and walked up

six flights of stairs in Greenwich Village
to beat the bloke up. And Nels

had travelled all the way from Chicago to do it.
How happy, I thought, Nels would have been

here at the Casino where Aussies stroll drugged
day and night, clutching drinks

and sucking cigarettes, hypnotized
by the machines—even the tossed

Heads or Tails a subject of high fever.
He adored every pony

he lost on. Addicted to poker, he never won
in his life—except for seducing my first wife.

I followed him that year, too dumb
to figure out it was not me he was so fond of.

There's still sting left in old wounds.
"How did he die?" asks my friend,

but all I know is that Nels died
in Sag Harbor, after he gave up at last

on Chicago, cursed "the second city" because
it had become more Saul Bellow's town than his.

Alas, what a terrible mistake it's been
to know only writers. "I don't know

any people," a poet told me, "I'm
only a writer." Today, though,

my fellow writer is paying for lunch
and we're not reviewing each other's books

or seducing each other's wives. I smile big
and think Maybe, just Maybe, I can be friends

with a writer after all, far from America,
every inch of the wide Pacific essential.

Francis Webb Reflects on His Failures

They did nothing for me, though I was obliged
to thank them. *Gracias por Nada*, I snarled,
unconvincing. *Panaceas por Nada*, that's what

they had. Yet they ignored first flower in months
though it glowed before them. And they heard
nothing, knew nothing. In my mind the hot tree

roared. When the hurly-burly was done
I, like Theresa in confinement, languished,
wove my own web, caught a wee poem now and then.

In the medical medieval grim fortress the seasons
chilled my walls or burned them. My friend
the spider prospered. On Christmas I rocked

a wee Christ-child of a poem on its pale sheet.
I had my Christ-child. Man had his Hydrogen Bomb,
outside the walls of any asylum. "Sane" man

cuddled his bomb. I wanted no visit from those
who assaulted the earth, had no pity
on this species and that, not even themselves.

Christmas, I said, should be *a hushed time,*
sacred lull, recollection entered softly—
not noise and assault, potlatch of who-

can-give-most, though rarely of Self. I scared
off old friends, had no visit. Like Gerard
I brooded. They studied my charts,

claimed their cure calmed me. My first cheery
thought, I confessed on a couch,
concerned spider orchids—a bright lovely group

in light breeze, blue-inked on pink.
Wordsworth might have dropped his daft daffodils
had he seen these near my cell. A circlet

of dew had fallen around them—globules, worlds—
each shining and, I think, spinning.
Dr. Heal relented that once, opened the gates—

a *tentative* cure, so he said. I shook hands,
bobbed and kowtowed my gratitude.
It was not snarly then. But what did I find,

once released? I had dreamed of my own Eden—
a flatlet on Darling Road, a few books,
food out of tins, my Brahms and Prokofiev, Beethoven.

Madness! Nothing but madness out there.
Altars to Pizza, Espresso, Gin. Neon throbbing
to false gods, tarmac where trees had been.

I grieved every loss. Then I was gaoled
for putting my foot through a television,
was returned as absconder. No one asked me

what I had kicked out, or *whom.*
It's crazy to sit watching as if chained,
welcome trash into the mind, day after day.

This time, I became your obedient servant
spacing the pills. But help they did not.
Only the salesman was helped. When I heard

a great spirit, his music, I thought,
"They'd have locked him up too."
With mind numbed I perceived *it was prayer*

and simple faith that held every clue.
Time mooched along. Major events
were "porridge, not cornflakes one morning,"

"a box of matches for free from a nurse."
Days beat out their dumb and numb toneless tune
"as if from an out-of-date pianola," so I said

in a note smuggled out. Up before seven,
a step out on dark grass, then tea. One bird
with inspired eye watched me eat. Seagulls

soared up from the river—no other visit
all season. Their music was too squawky modern
for me, and I told them so. Sun was Samson

rounding his mill wheel monotonous. At night
a star now and then shone, but was not
compassionate—no more than you, Sirs.

"A cold star would wink at me, then be wiped off
the sky by a cloud rag. There's nothing moving
but prayer," (I quote myself, Sirs). I felt myself

a new Nicodemus born of my hell. The doctors
chained me for more torture, and I thought
"Fine, at least that will be pain. I will feel it."

To be vertically down was my chief sin against Self,
others as well. I dreamed man was ringed round
by wee creatures, judged by them. They asked

if he deserved to survive, the way he's used earth.
"And us!" argued some. Another—mere ghost of the cock
that had crowed for our Lord—spoke like a man now.

He reviewed man's monstrous inventions.
"Let him die, who did this again and again,"
called out the creatures, cacophonous rage!

"No," cried the passionate rooster, the ghost.
"Here and there we find, if we seek closely,
pockets of goodness, though mostly obscure—

A clean sweep of fire would catch all—
even such goodness. And therefore we'll spare them
in the spirit of Him who forgave Simon Peter."

Though outvoted, this chanticleer voice made his ruling.
The world would spin on as it had, with me in my cell
hunched in the long night composing until my last word

flew out of my lips with dawn breaking
and the world trembling as if for the first time with its mercy.
I pray for pockets of good, even within men who are
        monsters.

Elegy for Grace

At Alcatraz the convicts
were not allowed cold showers
lest they were shaping up
to survive cold waters of the Bay.
And in Australia a poet
tells us the adventures
of her father, who was a doctor
in the prison at Berrima.
Saltpeter in their food
took care of their sex problems,
she said, and now and then
euthanasia was an approach
to a troublesome convict.
Then she showed us through
her Federation stone house
stock-full of antiques—
the gifts of dying patients—
some convicts, some not—
heirlooms now. It seemed
a good way to get rich,
a medical career in Australia.
And all I could do to keep up
with a few of her fabulous odd
facts was one I had found
in the *Times*. "Embalmers these days
need far less formaldehyde
than they did in the past,
for our bodies are full
of preservatives—all
salted down like fish
for the long voyage."
We all bear in our bones

the scentless balm
of civilization. Grace stoops
to fetch a box
of fine silver from under
the four-poster bed,
fee from a terminal case,
and her half-dingo dog
goes for me like Cerberus snarling,
the same dog that took a chunk
out of A. D. Hope's leg.
Next morning we strolled around
the high walls
of that prison, then joked
with a guard. "You can visit," he said,
"but if you do, you'll never get out."
We demurred, journeyed on
as if pardoned, reprieved, given a ticket
of leave. And soon after, we mourned
Grace—that tall oak of a woman who had shared
her penultimate evening with us,
said good-bye as she stood
trembling in moonlight.

A Few for the Peacock Outside My Window

I.

Peacock, every time you stroll past
I move back a few million years,
watch your scaly claw clutching mud.

And it's not clear which careful print
will make you immortal, outlast
sapphires, emeralds, vainglorious cry.

The shadows grow long in my life too.

II.

The woman comes close, stares at you
as if at jewels in a window.
And as I stare at her it seems odd

not to have the same freedom you do,
and to caw out aloud right after.
No wonder my sad feathers drag

across brick. You know nothing of this.

III.

All day long you pace about, stretch
your blue neck, appear to gaze intently
yet you ignore the Japanese girl

who jumps up and down to get your attention.
In fact, you notice nothing, are pure
projection—a blank field for imagination.

I imagine you my friend, plump with empathy.

IV.

Notice me! Take pity upon me! Is that not
what I have said to so many? And is that
not your game too, though pretending indifference?

Because you're the center all day and night
in this courtyard you may well think
they adore you dearly, think of nothing but you.

But peacock, you're not even found in their book.

V.

In thousands of snapshots your vanity rules
and you're passed from hand to hand.
Oh, you were a wonder, priceless,

greater than all else they paid to see.
In distant countries you bring smiles
to their faces, like love remembered.

Yet you gave nothing but your mindless shriek.

VI.

One more day we are close, you and I
while I fretfully prepare my departure.
How I too would like to stay, centered,

not far to stroll. Yet most of all I envy
your emptiness—your inane enthusiasm
for nothing but sun at your feet.

Peace of mind is to know nothing, to glow.

VII.

Negative capability—a term we reserve
for when far too much floods our minds
and thoughts are at war, civil war raging.

But with you the term can be used
with pure meaning—as nothing's in your
small head, not one word rattling around.

Yet no past year troubles you. No face tortures.

VIII.

Wisdom equals that quite negative ability—
emptiness you seem to have achieved
with your mindlessness, which we must work for.

In a cave I could do it, in the tenth year
of mantras, when my longing for those
who have tortured me would begin to subside.

Then we would be equals—two empty minds glowing.

The Peacocks

The sight of a feather in a peacock's tail, whenever I gaze at it, makes me sick!

—Charles Darwin

Transfixed, the people stand and gaze
at peacocks, they're not sure quite why.

It's something vaguely sexual, they think,
as they watch and nudge one another, say

"Maybe he'll do it again," then fall silent.
This is altogether too mysterious

and deadly serious a business. Now and then
the male stands, apparently indifferent,

while the peahen walks idly around him,
as if utterly unconcerned, not noticing

the plumage, how his feathers unfurl
with a shuddery rattle and his blue neck

glows more iridescent than ever.
She merely pecks in this crack and that,

or pretends to, circling around him.
Then for a moment she is mounted. Not much

to that! Quickly over and done with
and done again! Hardly enough occasion

for all this brightness. Yet the people gaze
as if at a wonder, worth selling tickets for,

as if they have something to believe in after all
other than their own un-noteworthy rituals

which will somehow get conducted between dusk and dawn
and give them enough of a glow to get through one more day.

BAD BOG

The program's on "Bad Bogs,"
how to get out of—if you're stuck
in the outback—how to get back
on track, get your wheels unstuck

and the rest of you too. It seems
there are ways of pulling yourself
out of quicksand, using nothing
but a rope and your own
ingenuity. (Who has a rope?)

There are times
when your engine has failed—
when all you can do is fix up
some shade and lie in it,
careful not to use up
any energy. (Who has energy?)

There are times when shade
of your hat's just a start.
(Use mud on the rest of you.)

There are times when a stick
can dig you out, Man—
out of the worst mess
                            you ever got in.
(Who's got a stick?)

There are times, Mate,
when a lizard's the best
friend you've had,
                            ever.
(Who's had a friend?)

There are times when you boil
the swamp in your billy,
find it's just fine.

Look for nuggets, rattle
                    your cup. Note
that lizard's blue tongue.
Send up some smoke.

Next time, bring a C.B.
Or don't go at all—
not to the outback,
                    not to the bush.

IN A SHOP IN AUSTRALIA

The Japanese gentleman asks where he might see
kangaroos. You'd think from his big eyes
he referred to a mythical beast,
one seldom seen—like the Loch Ness monster
or a griffin, survivor from classical times.

"There's a paddock down below the town,"
the shopkeeper tells him. "They'll be there
at dusk. No way you can miss them."

The gentleman stocks up on film—enough
for thousands of kangaroos. And just
to be safe, an armful of roos stuffed
with cotton. And a few koalas, teddy bears

to take back to Mt. Fuji. Later I envy
his faith, how he must sit alert on the tour bus
scanning the bush, every scorched tree
and the carpet of ash not unlike Hiroshima.

The Marlboro Man of Australia

A millionaire crooner of Westerns
is our profile this evening—cute dimples, cleft
chin, notes the woman who interviews him,
who asks if his good looks help in his trade.

She feels his biceps, declares them impressive.
He's used to such flirtations, fields such lust
as hers in good humor. And he's not bad
at strumming his guitar, mounting his horse

like the Marlboro man. The resemblance to Elvis
is noted, an asset for sure. He'll go far,
already has—for he was born to a vast holding,
and his cattle roam far over Queensland.

He's an Adonis with talent, only in
his mid-twenties—decades ahead of nothing
but fame, success more than assured.
He's got a contract in hand from America,

tour overseas planned. He may star in films
but at the moment wants to stay close
to the land—a few days at home and he's clean
again. He loves the fresh air, horses, vast space.

He's too good to be true, the awed mistress
of this interview concludes. She envies, she says,
his flawless skin, how does he do it?
And his voice is not bad, he knows lots of songs.

But before leaving off he wants to divulge
another ambition—to go into politics—

"to STOP IMMIGRATION." He says it with grit
on his teeth. It's his obsession, a life mission.

"If that's what it takes, I'll do it," he vows.
"We should never give up our birthright.
A man's land is his most precious possession."
And he was born to a great deal of it indeed.

Let's not mention Aboriginals, chased from that land.
Nor consider the homeless, huddled in holds
of creaking boats, touching inhospitable shores.
Feed them to sharks, would suggest
                    the political Marlboro man.

A Familiar News Item

A pit bull kills a small boy,
and is promptly "put down"—

no more to play beneath the clothesline
where the mother turned away

for only a moment. The father,
interviewed for the six o'clock news,

says he cannot blame the dog.
It was a good dog he had,

and a good son. He'll miss them both.
(Grief takes a thousand and one forms

is my thought.) For a few days
there's talk of banning the dogs

as after the Strathfield massacre
there was talk of banning the guns—

good for nothing but hunting people.
But within a few days all is back to normal

and the do-nothings again are in charge.
TV offers a program showing how gentle

pit bulls can be. They are shown doing tricks,
fetching the ball back. One owner puts meat

in his own mouth, gets down on all fours,
lets the dog take a bite. A marvelous dog!

A marvelous semiautomatic rifle! And besides,
the toll's not all that great. Beats boredom!

A great nation needs to prove itself through waste
of life—one by one into the fire with them.

The Exile at Midmorning

On an antipodean bus I look about
and witness those who would be
companions of my exile. One picks
his nose. Another preens
the left horn of his mustache,
slicked with wax. A girl drills
her ear out with her gimlet finger,
then finds a sweet, deep in her purse.

She wears pink ballet slippers.
I look away through rain, check
building fronts—mostly yellow,
ochre, nipple brown—and the same
drab signs as those at home.
Midas Muffler, for instance, is here—
and Burger King and Pizza Hut.
I've come full circle, maybe.
The bus leads nowhere special.

I get down and walk and the rain
is good against my face,
not hot tears at all. Grief's
washed out. In Venice the letter
never came, though I stood waiting.
Streets were made of the sea's
long filthy fingers. Not once
did I allow myself so much
as a treat of one cappuccino or cognac.
Day after day I came to the post office cage,
was told *Niente*, nothing for me,
another kick in the teeth.

We give up our griefs like dead grass
yielding to wind. Even the smallest root
clings as long as it can.
One hair, then another, an agon
each time. And that is the job
also of the wind and the rain
and the sea and its long filthy fingers.

Homo Delphinus

Born in Russia, we are told, and yet we see them
through the porthole of TV, here in Australia,
cavorting for the cameras placed under water—
more ballet than swimming. Then they walk
through that water with closed-mouth smiles,

a mask of ecstasy, and not coming up for air—
not yet. Born from the watery womb-world into water,
they are eased into this life. At last they rise
to the breast, cradle of arms. There is, after all,
on earth such a joy, and they are set upon its course.

And we who watch can hardly grasp this antipode
of all we have known. When we first touched our world
we drew back as if plunged into fire, and we soon
tasted ash. Birth underwater will ease the transition
and their lives may be gentler than ours. There's no need

for slaps on the buttocks, to warn them of hard times ahead.
We are told they are fearless, immune to most pain, slow
to learn fear. And are not hostile! In that case,
will they defend life and limb? Or be easy prey for a tiger
or Hitler? Does our distrust not save us? Should we not pity

the children born without quills or instinct to make missiles?
And if it is true, as optimists hope, that they will clean up
the earth left oozing with garbage (and not foul it more),
they'll have full employment. Or perhaps they are not for this
world, not equipped for such hell. They may be more
    dolphins

than humans. Their faces are benign, as if they will all
become saints. I would join if I could their circle of bliss.
We would dance into fire, and never fear loss of our souls.
Though these aliens may perish of trust, I will bless them
and fall into their arms drifting wide to hug and kiss and
     comfort me.

Tableaux

In the museum I leaned forward
for a better look at our parlor—
preserved just as we had left it,
or almost. The girl's needlepoint
they had hung in a frame down the hall
and a bonnet my wife wore on shipboard
for some reason was placed
on a mannikin dressed all in black.
But amazing—how vivid the scene—
with rocking chairs ready to rock
and tea service laid out, and books
brought from England stacked neatly.
On top was the same text I left off,
Paradise Lost, open, I see,
to the ninth book. Leaning close,
over the rope, I conclude that Satan
is still falling from heaven—
No more shall he sit and partake
of chummy discourse with God
or enjoy the rural repast served
up above. Just then the guard appears,
with her extreme disapproval. "Sir!"
she exclaims, "You set off the alarm,
Step back! Step back!" From my own
parlor, how dare she! I have lost
home and birthright, have been roped off
from my own hearth. Damn her!
Then we stroll down the hall, past
the Aboriginal family standing and gazing
aghast and bereft at their cave as it was
eons ago, their hands outspread
like abandoned gloves on the stone.

First Trip to Rottnest Island

Perched in Perth, caught
between desert and sea, we had
to edge out yet farther—hence
this balmy-breezed island, not quite
Antarctica, not quite Arcadia.
An island for only seven thousand years,
yet ancient enough for us—
old promontory offshore now,
wave-beaten. It has
given lush flowers to Kew,
and its convicts can be found
in the churchyard. I pause
to consider the palimpsest
of stone—names scrawled as graffiti
on walls left for others. Children
lasted not long—dozens fell in a season.
Strolling and wheeling our bikes
we wonder where the whiff
of fresh bread comes from.
A double row
of Moreton Bay figs
has been proposed for an avenue.
No ghosts are in sight—no clank
of chains, no sight of a man
bent under the cat o' nine, bleeding.
Altogether, Rottnest
is idyllic, Edenic—
as far as we can go before
we curl back on ourselves.
We can sink down in relative peace
for the night, unroll our swag.
At least the nest is not rotten today.

CHRISTMAS CARD FROM AUSTRALIA

The Christmas tree here is a parasite
that clamps its roots onto another's,
a perfectly innocent fig or a pine.

Its blossoms are golden,
hanging like curls, and maybe not
even blossoms. Some sort of mistletoe,

but at least they are bright and cited
as evidence that the Antipodes are not
entirely abandoned, lacking in holidays

every respectable nation deserves.
In fact, there's a frenzy of buying
just as wild as that in any state

of our rightside-up Union. The poor
are still poor with their envious eyes
and the sum total of woe, Christmas day,

is greater than all the much-
advertised joy. Christmas is still
Christmas, though, glittering day when we each

are found lacking, whether topside or keel's
heel. The brilliant gold of that tree
dazzles and I'm looking around for Santa.

LEAVING OZ

I have given a child our potted geranium
and she has carried it off to her mother.

The kangaroo paws have withered
and my boomerang's packed away in the roll-on.

They say it takes seven years to adjust
to such an exile as we have chosen this season,

and I feel that I don't have that option.
No one wants us, if the truth be told.

So we will wander back to America,
strangest country of all. A tourist

opens fire on the White House
but a spokesman says the President was never

in any danger. No more than usual!
There is nothing to be done about our guns—

just import more. This one's from China.
Let's stroll the Swan's bank for another

sunset of crimson, maybe the last day
we won't get assassinated or our plane downed.

And the shrimper's children can give us
their farewell blessing as the dark comes down.

INDEX OF FIRST LINES

ABOUT THE AUTHOR

David Ray is the author of several books of poetry, including *Wool Highways and Other Poems* (Helicon Nine Editions, 1993) and *The Tramp's Cup* (Chariton Review Press, 1978), both of which received the Poetry Society of America's William Carlos Williams Award; *Not Far from the River* (Copper Canyon Press, 1990); *The Maharani's New Wall* (Wesleyan University Press, 1989), which was nominated for a Pulitzer Prize; and *Sam's Book* (Wesleyan University Press, 1988), which won the Maurice English Poetry Award. Ray has also had fiction, essays, and poetry published in many journals, and received a National Endowment for the Arts award for his fiction. He is presently a professor of English at the University of Missouri–Kansas City.

Colophon

Design and typography by Tim Rolands
Cover and title page by Teresa Wheeler, NMSU designer

Text and display are set in Monotype Centaur,
designed by Bruce Rogers, 1912–1914.

Printed and bound by Edwards Brothers, Ann Arbor, Michigan
Distributed by Thomas Jefferson University Press,
Kirksville, Missouri